exploding ants

Amazing Facts About How Animals Adapt

To Katherine, Daniel, Ethan, Willie, and Chris, lovers of nature and future writers.—J. S.

The drawing on the jacket, title page, and page 18 is reproduced from Hermann: *Defensive Mechanisms in Social Insects,* fig. 7-26, copyright © 1984 by Praeger Publishers. Reproduced with permission of Greenwood Publishing Group, Inc. Westport CT.

Atheneum Books for Young Readers

An imprint of Simon & Schuster Children's Publishing Division

1230 Avenue of the Americas

New York, New York 10020

Text copyright © 1999 by Joanne Settel

Book design by Patti Ratchford

The text of this book is set in Joanna Monotype

Printed in Hong Kong

First Edition

10 9 8 7 6 5 4 3 2 1

Library of Congress Cataloging-in-Publication Data

Settel, Joanne.

Exploding ants : amazing facts about how animals adapt / by Joanne Settel.—1st ed.

p.   cm.

Includes bibliographical references and index.

Summary: Describes examples of animal behavior that may strike humans as disgusting, including the "gross" ways animals find food, shelter, and safety in the natural world.

ISBN 0-689-81739-8

1. Animal behavior—Juvenile literature. [1. Animals—Habits and behavior.] I. Title.

QL751.5.S54   1998

591.5—dc21

97-35395   CIP   AC

FIRST
EDITION

exploding ants

Amazing Facts About How Animals Adapt

BY JOANNE SETTEL, Ph.D.

Atheneum Books for Young Readers

contents

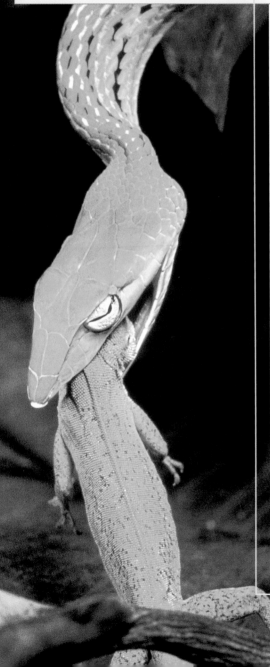

why animals do gross things

Animals often do things that seem gross to us. They eat foods that people would find nauseating. They make their homes in disgusting places and feed on mucus and blood. They swell or blow up their body parts.

But while these behaviors are nasty to us, they are critical to life on earth. They make it possible for many kinds of living things to find food, shelter, and safety. Different species make use of every possible space and gobble down every nutritious crumb of food in the natural world. If every species of animal ate the same kind of food, or lived in the same place, there simply wouldn't be enough to go around. It would become impossible for all of the species to survive. So instead, animals specialize. One predator eats flesh, while another feeds on blood.

As a result, when it comes to eating, nothing is wasted. Almost every part of every living animal, from skin to dung to mucus, can provide food for some other species. All of these things contain good nutrients. An animal that has the right digestive organs and chemicals can easily break them down.

Similarly, when it comes to finding shelter, animals make use of any hole or space or building material that they can find. For example, the smelly, slimy holes and organs inside the body of a bigger animal can often provide a warm, protective home for small animals like insects.

Finally, animals often put their body parts to good use. Animals don't have bags to carry things around, tools to open things, knives to cut things, or weapons to defend themselves. Instead, they use their own bodies in ways that seem gross to us. By stretching, swelling, and bursting open, they can trick predators, store food, swallow big gulps, and defend their nests.

fooled ya

a disgusting disguise

That slimy black-and-white lump that looks like a bird dropping may actually be alive! It could really be a swallowtail butterfly *larva*, a caterpillar that copies or *mimics* the colors and shape of a dropping to avoid getting eaten by predators. To make its disguise more realistic, the caterpillar also holds its body in the shape of a dropping and rests motionlessly on a leaf.

Though it looks gross to humans, the caterpillar's appearance serves it well. Because it looks unappetizing, the larva doesn't need to hide from predators. Hungry animals will see it and move on, searching for something that seems more like food.

The swallowtail caterpillar doesn't spend its whole life looking like a dropping. After fifteen days of growing and developing, it spins itself a cocoon. Then, around ten days later, it emerges as a beautiful, brightly colored butterfly.

This swallowtail butterfly larva has the shape and colors of a bird dropping.

DAVID M. DENNIS

8

fatal flashes

A male firefly flashing in search of a friendly female may be in for a nasty surprise. The flash he gets in response could be from a predatory female of a different species, looking for a meal instead of a mate!

When male fireflies flash their lights, they are seeking a mate of their own kind. There are over nineteen hundred species of fireflies worldwide. In any one location, there may be dozens of different firefly species busily flashing. Normally, the different firefly species can tell each other apart, because each has its own special pattern of short and long flashes. A male will signal and then wait to see a female of his species flash the correct response. A male *Photinus pyralis*, for example, looks for a flash that comes exactly two seconds after his own. When he sees the signal he flies toward the flashing female and checks her out with his antennae. Only if she is really one of his own species will he mate with her.

Sometimes, however, unsuspecting males are tricked by the flashes of predatory females. These females can imitate the flash patterns of other species. They use their special skills to lure in males. Then, before the males have a chance to check them out, the females attack. Instead of finding mates, the unlucky males find themselves trapped in the *mandibles*, or jaws, of a hungry predator.

This predatory female firefly holds a male with her legs as she gobbles him up, headfirst.
JAMES E. LLOYD

murderous nest mates

Sharing a nest with a newly hatched cuckoo bird can be a deadly proposition. Cuckoo young aren't big on sharing. In fact, they make certain that they won't have to share food or space by throwing their nest mates out of the nest.

Cuckoos are nest stealers, or *brood parasites*. These European, Asian, and African birds lay their eggs in the nests of other species. The female cuckoo searches for a host bird who is busy laying her own eggs. She waits until the host female leaves the nest to feed. Then the cuckoo sneaks in, pushes out one host egg, and lays her own.

When the host female returns, everything looks normal. The number of eggs in the nest is the same as when she left. In addition, the cuckoo egg is similar in color and size to her own. Not knowing that one egg is the cuckoo's, the host bird sits on or *incubates* all the eggs to keep them warm.

It takes at least two weeks before the host bird's eggs begin to hatch. The cuckoo's egg, however, is designed to hatch after only twelve days, before the others. This gives the young cuckoo a perfect opportunity to rid itself of any competitors.

Soon after hatching, the young cuckoo does its deadly deed. It rolls the eggs of its nest mates out of the nest. If it misses any of the eggs and they do hatch, the cuckoo pushes the baby birds out as well.

Now the cuckoo nestling has its foster parent all to itself. The young invader grows rapidly, until it is much bigger than its host. Unaware that the cuckoo is not her offspring, the host mother puts all her energy into feeding this big baby. The job is so difficult that the host mother often loses weight in the process. Meanwhile, the cuckoo mother is long gone, having left all the work of parenting to someone else.

A warbler feeds a large cuckoo chick. The young cuckoo has pushed all of the warbler's own eggs and chicks out of the nest.

A. J. KNYSTAUTAS/VIREO

invasion of the body snatchers

the brainwashers

A worm reprogramming an ant's brain may sound like the stuff of science fiction. But that's what really happens when the small liver fluke gets itself inside an ant. The tiny wormlike fluke is a *parasite* that spends different parts of its life inside the bodies of three different host animals: a snail, an ant, and a sheep. The fluke must get inside each host by being eaten. It uses its amazing reprogramming skills to get itself into the mouth of a hungry sheep.

Liver flukes actually begin their lives inside a snail. The snail starts things off when it eats some sheep dung filled with liver fluke eggs. Inside the snail, the eggs hatch, releasing thousands of tiny larvae (young flukes). As many as six thousand mucus-covered fluke larvae then gather together into a squirming ball. Eventually the snail ejects this grape-sized glob from its body.

The next step in the fluke's life cycle takes place when an ant feeds on the mucus ball. This brings the larvae into the ant's stomach, where they bore into the stomach wall. Most of the larvae remain here and grow into adult flukes.

One larva, however, doesn't hang around in the stomach wall. It has a special mission.

This larva must make sure that its fellow flukes can get from the ant to a sheep. This is no easy matter. Sheep don't normally eat ants; they feed on grass. Somehow the fluke must get the sheep to swallow a fluke-infested ant along with the grass. One way to do this is to change the ant's behavior. The special larva carries out its mission by burrowing into the ant's brain. Once this happens, the ant begins to act in a really bizarre way.

Normally, ants scurry around on the ground in search of food. Hidden beneath the grass, these ants are safe from the jaws of munching sheep. "Brainwashed" ants climb to the tip of a blade of grass and cling to it. The ants remain there, motionless, for hours. As a result, grazing sheep can readily chomp them down.

This brings the fluke to its final home, the sheep's liver. Here the parasite matures into a leaf-shaped adult and lays its eggs. The sheep soon *excretes*, or gets rid of, these eggs with its dung. Then, along comes a hungry snail, and the process starts all over again.

This adult liver fluke, which lives inside a sheep's liver, has both male and female parts in its body. The dark structures at the top are ovaries, which produce eggs. The pink branches are testes, which produce sperm.

ARMED FORCES INSTITUTE OF PATHOLOGY

caterpillar guts for breakfast

The living, breathing body of a caterpillar is the perfect nest and food source for the larva of a *braconid wasp*. A newly hatched braconid larva feasts on the caterpillar's guts, as it grows safe and sound under the host animal's skin.

Braconid wasps, as well as a number of other species of tiny wasps and flies, are known as *parasitoids*. They feed on other living organisms or hosts, slowly killing them in the process. Because parasitoids are very, very small (less than one-half inch long), they don't need a large host. A nice juicy caterpillar, beetle, or cricket can provide a little parasitoid with all the food it requires.

The first trick for a parasitoid is to get its eggs inside the host. Females of different species have developed many ways to sneak their eggs into living animals. Some lay their eggs on their host's favorite food plant. The eggs are then eaten and hatch inside the host's stomach. Other females drop their eggs onto the outside of a host. The larvae hatch and then burrow into the host's skin. Braconid wasp females carry a sharp needle or *ovipositor*, which they use to inject eggs right into the body of the host.

Once inside a host, such as a caterpillar, the parasitoid larva is surrounded by food. But the larva can't just munch away at its living food source. Some parasitoids need to mature inside their host for as long as ten days. During this time, the little larva must keep its host alive, to provide a steady supply of fresh food.

One parasitoid fly, the *tachinid* larva, does this through careful feeding. First, the larva feeds on the caterpillar's blood. Later, the growing tachinid begins to feed on the rest of its host, slowly killing it in the process. At this point, the hungry larva produces a chemical which turns the host's tissues into a thick brown liquid. The larval fly then slurps up this caterpillar juice for several more days while it grows into an adult.

After a week or two of feeding and growing, parasitoid wasp or fly larvae are ready to pop out through the skin of their dead or dying hosts. While parasitoid flies are now fully mature and simply fly away, parasitoid wasps aren't quite ready to leave. The little wasps cover their host with a mass of tiny white cocoons. The body of one host caterpillar can hold as many as two thousand of them!

Inside the cocoons, the wasps now enter a pupal stage. Like butterflies, these little insects *hibernate* for five to ten days as they mature into adults. Eventually, the tiny, fully grown wasps emerge and the body of their host is simply left behind.

The deadly behavior of parasitoids plays an important role in controlling populations of other insects. Scientists have been able to use parasitoids to kill insect pests that destroy food crops such as sugarcane and fruit.

Tiny wasps have built their cocoons on the body of this living tomato hornworm. The hornworm's body provides them with both food and shelter.

ENTOMOLOGICAL SOCIETY OF AMERICA

swelling, expanding, and exploding bodies

living honey jars

The swollen sacs of nectar that hang from the roof of a honey ant nest are actually alive. They're the fat bodies of ants that have turned themselves into living honey jars.

The "honey jars" are worker ants that store food and are known as *repletes*. Repletes spend their lives hanging upside down from the roof of their nest waiting to feed or be fed. Their bodies provide sterile, airtight food containers.

It is when the colony has lots of extra food that the repletes get fed. Each replete receives regurgitated or spit-up food from hundreds of ordinary worker ants. The food consists of a golden liquid filled with a predigested mix of termite parts and plant nectar.

As they take in more and more food, the repletes swell. Soon their rear ends or abdomens are as large as small grapes. The swollen ants then climb to the roof of the nest and con-

tinue to eat. They remain on the roof for months, hanging by their claws, barely able to move. If for some reason a replete falls down, other workers must help it drag its large, balloonlike body back up to the ceiling.

When food supplies outside the nest run low, the repletes become the feeders. Hungry nest mates now gather round for food. They touch the repletes' antennae with their own. The repletes then regurgitate big drops of golden honey.

The extra food provided by the repletes is important to colony survival. Honey ants live in large colonies in dry desert regions of North America, Africa, and Australia, where food is often scarce. Storing food in their living honey jars enables the colony to make it through the hottest, driest desert seasons.

The sweet "honey" of the honey ant repletes is not only food for other ants, but also for some people. The Aborigines in Australia consider the swollen honey ants to be sweet treats and pop them into their mouths like candy.

(Left and center) These swollen honey ants cling to the roof of their nests.

(Right) A honey ant replete regurgitates nectar to a nest mate.

DR. JOHN R. CONWAY/ UNIVERSITY OF SCRANTON

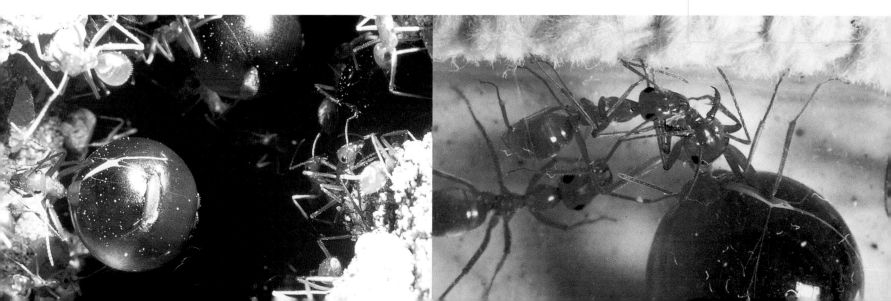

exploding ants

Soldier ants of the species *Camponotus saundersi* are designed to explode. These ants make themselves burst to defend their colony from other invading insects. When the ants explode, they spray out a sticky chemical that kills or glues their opponents in place.

Camponotus ants manufacture their deadly chemicals inside their own bodies. The chemicals are stored in two big sacs called *mandibular glands*. These glands take up most of the ant's body, opening just under the mandibles or jaws.

When an intruder approaches, the *Camponotus* ant will release small amounts of its special chemical to warn away the invader. If the intruder actually attacks, however, the *Camponotus* ant takes the next step. It violently contracts, or tightens, its muscles, bursting open and spewing out its deadly chemicals.

Camponotus ants aren't the only insects with this unusual behavior. It turns out that soldiers of the termite species *Globitermes sulfureus* are also exploders, bursting open when threatened and spraying a sticky yellow liquid all over their opponents.

This swelling ant is about to explode.

18

ballooning birds

A frigate bird with a swollen red throat isn't sick; it's just a male courting a mate. The male frigate has an incredibly stretchy sac, or pouch, on his throat. He uses this sac as a part of a spectacular mating display, designed to get the attention of females.

The frigate bird is a large black fisheater that nests in colonies on the seacoast. During the breeding season, the male frigate undergoes a dramatic change. His pale pink throat sac turns blood red. When the male is ready to display, he fills this sac with air. After thirty minutes of filling, the sac looks like a big red balloon.

The large-beaked frigate can keep his puffed-up throat inflated for hours at a time. He shows off its bright color by raising his beak to the sky, flapping his wings, and uttering a high-pitched cry.

A male frigate bird will continue this puffing and calling for several weeks. If he attracts a mate, he will then use his balloon-like throat to threaten other males that approach his nest. Once the female has laid an egg, the male stops threatening. Then the red sac fades back to a pale pink color.

Dramatic as the throat display is, it doesn't always work. A male frigate bird, however, isn't easily discouraged. If he doesn't attract a female on his first outing, he'll fly off to another nest site and try again.

The throat pouch of this frigate bird is puffed up like a balloon. Its bright colors will be used to attract females and threaten other males.
U.S. FISH AND WILDLIFE SERVICE

dog mucus and other tasty treats

a very slimy supper

The mucus in the nose of a dog may not sound like an inviting place to live. But for tiny tongue worms it provides both food and a nice warm home.

Tongue worms are parasites that feed on mucus, blood, and body tissues of other animals. Usually less than half an inch long, tongue worms of different species find their food inside the noses and breathing passages of reptiles, birds, and mammals. One species, *Linguatula serrata*, prefers dogs. This tiny worm spends much of its adult life unnoticed, hanging by four sharp claws on the inside of a dog's nose. A female *Linguatula* may stay this way for over two years as she sucks up mucus and lays eggs.

Dog mucus is fine for adult tongue worms, but not for the young. Larval tongue worms must spend their early lives in other hosts. For *Linguatula*, the life cycle begins when a female tongue worm lays several million eggs inside a dog's nose. This soon makes the infected dog sneeze. The dog's sneeze sprays the eggs out into the air and onto nearby plants. Egg-covered plants are then eaten by *herbivores* (plant eaters) such as rabbits. The rabbit becomes the new host. Inside the rabbit's intestines, hundreds of tongue worm larvae soon hatch out from their eggs. Once out, these larvae drill through the rabbit's intestine and wiggle into the host's lungs or liver, where they feast on its tissues.

Sooner or later the infected host rabbit dies. Its wormy body is eaten by *carnivores* (meat eaters) such as dogs. Once inside the dog, the male and female tongue worm larvae make their way into the dog's nose. Here they feast on mucus and mate and lay eggs, starting the cycle all over again.

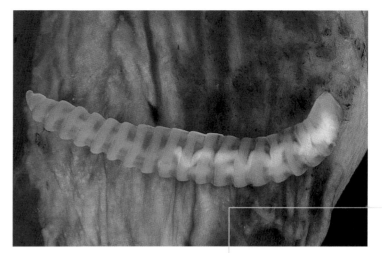

This very tiny tongue worm makes its home inside the mucus-filled passages of a dog's nose.

ARMED FORCES INSTITUTE OF PATHOLOGY

parasite pickers

When a wrasse fish wants a bite to eat, it swims into the waiting jaws of a large grouper or other waiting fish. Once inside, the wrasse gobbles up worms, bacteria, and other tiny organisms. Then the little wrasse simply swims back out and pokes around the larger fish's gills, fins, and skin. The wrasse is a cleaner. It is one of a number of small fish and shrimps that clean annoying organisms or parasites off big fish.

It might seem risky to be eating out of another fish's mouth, but the wrasse is in little danger. Though a predator, the larger fish never chomps down on its little visitor. Instead, it opens its mouth wide and puffs out its gills so that the wrasse can get inside. This relationship between the wrasse and the grouper and others is known as *symbiosis*.

Both animals benefit. The grouper gets cleaned of parasites and the wrasse gets a meal.

A grouper recognizes the cleaner by its special nodding swim and by its shape and color. The cleaner wrasse has a long, thin body with a black stripe running from head to tail. When a cleaner approaches, the grouper knows not to harm it.

Some fish, however, are designed to take advantage of this symbiotic relationship. The mimic blenny looks very much like a cleaner wrasse, but it is not a cleaner. By looking like the wrasse, the blenny can get close to a grouper. But instead of cleaning, the blenny rushes up and gets a meal by nipping off pieces of the grouper's flesh and fins.

The small wrasse cleans a lizard fish by eating tiny organisms that are found on its eye (or gills).

a mouthful from mom

When a mother gull wants to feed her young, she simply *regurgitates*, or throws up. Her waiting chicks then quickly gobble down a nice hunk of half-digested fish.

For the gull, regurgitating food is a handy way to deliver a meal. A mother gull may have to fly many miles from her nest to catch some fish. The easiest way to transport a load of food back home is in her stomach. As the mother gull flies, her stomach begins to break down the meal. By the time she reaches the nest, the food is already partly digested. This makes it easier for the chicks to get it into their small beaks.

When they are ready to eat, the nestlings beg for food by pecking at their mother's bill. This stimulates her to regurgitate a mouthful of fish into the nest.

Gulls aren't the only regurgitators. Many species of birds use this method to feed their young. But not all of them deposit their food into the nest. Some, such as finches, hummingbirds, and pigeons, drop a predigested mass right into the mouths or throats of their young. Others, such as pelicans, hold the regurgitated food in their gullets or throats. Then they open their large beaks really wide and allow the chicks to stick their heads right in and feed.

(Top) A young pelican pokes its head inside its mother's mouth in search of food. CRUICKSHANK/ VIREO.

(Center, bottom) An albatross and a morning dove regurgitate predigested food into the mouths of their waiting young.

ALBATROSS: MARK RAUZON/ U.S. FISH AND WILDLIFE SERVICE

DOVE: MIKE HOPIAK/CORNELL LABORATORY OF ORNITHOLOGY

sucking blood

bursting with blood

When a tick dines on blood, it fills and fills and fills. Like other bloodsuckers, such as fleas, mosquitoes, and bedbugs, a tick will gorge till it's nearly bursting with blood. After all, it's not always easy to find the next human, dog, or other juicy meal. So once a tick has found the perfect host, it sucks up all the blood its tiny body can hold.

Some ticks take in so much blood, they swell to nearly four times their normal size. That's like an adult human expanding to the height of a two-story building!

The advantage of slurping up a big meal is that the tick can go for months or even years without feeding. Still, in order to grow and develop normally, ticks must feed on blood during each step of their three-stage life cycle.

The life cycle, which can take months or years, begins when the tick hatches out of its egg. The larval tick crawls onto a bush or blade of grass and waits. If a host, such as a dog, passes by, the larva climbs aboard and searches for a good place to feed.

The larva begins feeding by pushing a sharp, dartlike mouthpart into its host's skin. Once it has firmly attached to the host, the larva starts filling with blood. The young tick then *molts*, or sheds its outer skin, and becomes a tiny eight-legged *nymph*. This freckle-sized nymph must suck down another blood meal

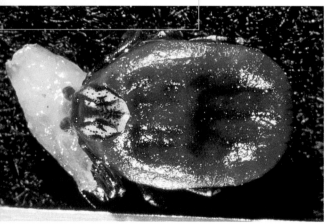

This fat American dog tick has just filled itself with blood.

ARMED FORCES INSTITUTE OF PATHOLOGY

before it can finish its development.

After feeding and growing, the nymph sheds its skin for the final time and pops out as an adult tick. This adult eats one more blood meal before it mates. Then, if it's a female, it finds a nice hidden spot and lays as many as six thousand eggs.

sticking around

A human scalp provides an ideal home and food source for a bloodsucking head louse. The tiny louse uses six clawed legs to permanently attach itself to the hair of its human host. Here it stays, while sucking up blood from the scalp every few hours. Safe within a forest of hair, the head louse grows, mates, and lays eggs. An adult female makes as many as three hundred eggs during her one-month life span. Using special cement-making glands, she glues these eggs to hairs. The eggs mature and hatch in about five days. The newly hatched young settle down on the scalp and suck up their first meal.

Although a hungry louse has plenty of food, it must cling tightly to its host. If it gets knocked off and loses its blood supply, the louse will die within two days. Humans who are infested usually carry around ten to twenty lice. While ordinary washing won't dislodge the little invaders, they can be removed by using special insect-killing shampoos or creams.

This head louse, which is less than one-fourth of an inch long, will spend most of its life clinging to a human hair.

ARMED FORCES INSTITUTE OF PATHOLOGY

a little blood between neighbors

Vomited blood may not sound like a tasty treat, but for vampire bats it can be a lifesaving meal. The tiny three-inch long mammals need to eat almost every night in order to stay alive. If a bat misses a meal, a little slurp of blood vomited up by a neighbor bat can be enough to keep it going until the next feed.

Vampire bats must share food because it's not always easy to get blood. First the bat must find a living host. Then it must be able to bite into its victim and slurp up blood without being noticed.

A hunt begins in the darkness of night, when the bat flies out from its roost. Using huge eyes and an excellent sense of smell, the bat picks out a sleeping animal, such as a cow or a horse.

Once it finds a living, breathing blood supply, the bat lands noiselessly and hops toward its victim on soft padded feet. The bat uses a special heat sensor in its nose to find a patch of warm blood vessels. Then it quickly cuts a tiny hole in its victim's skin with its razor-sharp teeth.

In about twenty minutes, the bat can lap up all the blood it needs. That's because the tiny one-ounce mammal only requires about two tablespoons of blood a day to stay strong and healthy. As the bat feeds, a special chemical in its saliva keeps the victim's blood from *clotting*, or forming a plug to stop blood flow.

The whole process of feeding requires speed and skill. The vampire bat must not only locate an animal to feed on, it must also take care not to wake its sleeping victim. Young bats don't always get it right. They are likely to miss at least one meal every fourteen days. But they aren't the only ones to get into trouble. Sometimes even mature bats miss a feed.

When a bat doesn't get to eat, it will return hungry to the tree or cave where it roosts with about twenty other bats. By licking the fur and lips of a well-fed roost mate, the starving bat signals that it needs food. If the bat is lucky, the neighbor will share its bloody stomach contents. This process of blood sharing is rarely a one-way street. Often a bat that gets fed on one night will be able to regurgitate and return the favor at another time. In this way, vampire bats support each other in the risky business of feeding on blood.

A vampire bat may share some of its blood meal with a hungry neighbor.

GERALD WILKINSON/ UNIVERSITY OF MARYLAND, COLLEGE PARK

an underwater bloodsucker

When a lamprey gets hungry, it sucks a hunk of blood and flesh from the side of a living fish. The eel-like lamprey is a jawless fish that spends part of its life as a parasite, firmly attached to and feeding off other fishes.

The lamprey is not parasitic for all of its life. It spends a number of years as a small, blind, wormlike larva. The small, toothless, lamprey larva burrows into mud, where it feeds on microscopic organisms called *plankton*.

After five to seven years as a larva, the lamprey changes, or *metamorphoses*, into its adult form. It grows two to three feet in length and develops its sucking mouth. Then it spends a year or more as a parasite fattening up on fish blood before it breeds and dies.

The adult lamprey's large, round mouth is specially designed for its bloodsucking lifestyle. The mouth has suckerlike lips, which can grip firmly onto the skin of a live fish. The mouth also contains a toothed tongue and sharp, pointed teeth that are used to scrape a hole into the host's flesh.

Once a lamprey has latched on it can begin to feed. By pumping water through its gills, the lamprey creates a suction to draw blood from its host. As in other species of bloodsucking animals, the lamprey's saliva contains a special anticlotting chemical. Normally blood forms a clot, or plug, to prevent excess blood flow out of an opened wound. The lamprey's saliva keeps the blood steadily flowing.

When the lamprey finishes feeding, it drops off its host. The victim may swim away, seemingly unharmed. The wound caused by the lamprey, however, can easily get infected and lead to death.

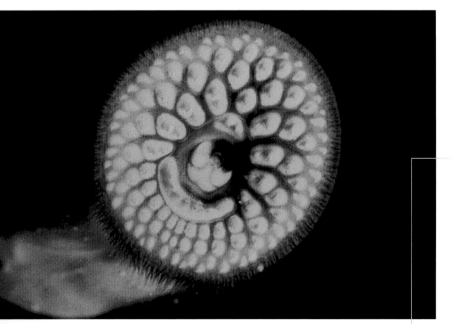

This parasitic lamprey has a large round sucking mouth that can be used to ream out flesh and blood from other live fish.

U.S. FISH AND WILDLIFE SERVICE

getting it down
a ball of bones

Every evening before it goes off to hunt, an owl spits up a few balls of fur and bones. The balls, or pellets, are what's left of the owl's last meal. An owl preys on small animals, such as mice, moles, shrews, birds, and insects. When the feathered predator captures its prey, it doesn't take the time to kill its victim and then pick out the fleshy, nutritious parts. It simply swallows the animal whole. Then the owl digests all the soft stuff, the muscles and organs. The rest, the fur, feathers, teeth, and bones, are wastes. The owl gets rid of these by regurgitating a pellet.

Owls normally spit up two pellets a day. Over time the pellets pile up and form large heaps under the owl's *roosting*, or resting, site. By examining these pellets, scientists can learn all about an owl's diet. A pellet of a barn owl, for example, usually contains entire skeletons of two or three mammals, lots of fur, and insect parts. That means that a barn owl gulps down around six small mammals a day.

Six small mammals at two to six ounces each seems like a lot of meat for a bird that weighs less than one pound. The twelve-ounce owl, however, doesn't get fat on this feast. Most of its food is just the fur and bones that get chucked up as round pellets.

(Top) A burrowing owl regurgitates a pellet of fur and bones.

MARY TREMAINE/CORNELL LABORATORY OF ORNITHOLOGY

(Center) A typical owl pellet is two to four inches in length.

(Bottom) This owl pellet has been picked apart. Inside are the skull

and bones of two small mouselike mammals, a vole and a shrew.

BARRY FRIEMAN

big, big gulps

Gulping down a whole pig or chicken may sound like an impossible task for a snake. But it's no big deal for a twenty-foot python. In fact, many snakes often swallow food much bigger than their own heads. Even very small snakes may feast on mice, rats, birds, frogs, and whole eggs.

The snake's ability to swallow big prey results from the special design of its jaw. The bones of its mouth are loosely joined to its skull. A stretchy strip of tissue called a *ligament* holds together the two halves of the lower jaw. When the snake swallows its din-

This long-nosed tree snake swallows a lizard headfirst.

DAVID M. DENNIS

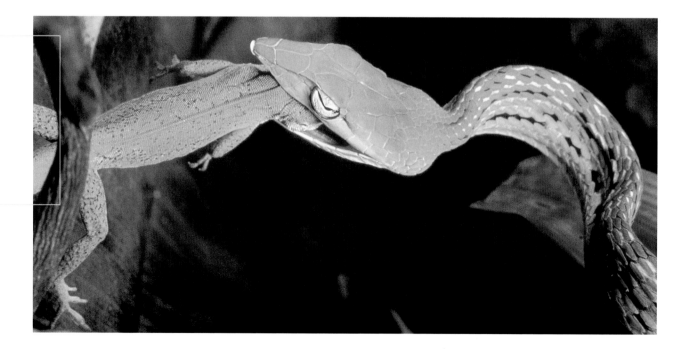

ner, its mouth can stretch wide open. The lower jawbones spread apart and each bone moves separately to pull the prey into the mouth.

Snakes generally try to gulp down their food headfirst. This causes the prey's legs to fold back as the snake swallows. In addition, the snake's sharp teeth are curved backward, preventing the squirming prey from wiggling back out. As the snake works its food down its throat, it pushes its windpipe out of its mouth. This means that it doesn't have to stop breathing as it swallows.

Because snakes eat such big meals, they don't need to eat every day. Most snakes only have to grab a meal once a week, and some only eat once every month. Large pythons hold the record, however. After feasting on a pig or chicken, these huge snakes can go for more than a year without any other food!

gulping eyeballs

Frogs use their bulging eyeballs not just to see their food but to swallow it as well. Frogs are meat eaters, or carnivores. They feed on any small creature that moves. This can include insects, spiders, worms, snails, fish, and even mice. Upon spotting an insect or other prey, a frog quickly shoots out its long, sticky tongue. The tongue flicks forward like a lasso, wrapping around and pulling a wiggly meal back into the frog's mouth. This whole operation takes less than one second.

Once the frog has captured its food, it wastes no time with chewing. Though many frogs have teeth, these are small and sharp and not designed for munching. Instead, the frog only uses its teeth to hold on to its victim and swallow it whole.

Swallowing can present a real challenge if the prey is alive and fairly large. A frog can use its front feet to help cram the food back into its mouth, but for the final push, it depends on its eyes. While our eyes are fixed in our heads in bony cups or *orbits*, a frog's eyes sit in orbits with no bottoms. So, when it swallows, the frog can close its eyelids and drop its eyeballs down into its mouth. Then the eyeballs can work as a team to push food into the throat toward the waiting stomach.

This African bullfrog will need to use its eyes to help it swallow a rat.

DAVID M. DENNIS

a smelly proposal

A sniff of urine sends an important message to a male rhinoceros. It tells him when a female is ready to mate. If the female is in *heat*, or in mating condition, her urine contains special chemicals called *pheromones*. When the male smells these pheromones, he knows he can approach her.

Sniffing female urine is a common behavior among male *ungulates*, or hoofed mammals including horses, deer, cattle, rhinos, and sheep. To get the full scent of a female's urine, the male performs a behavior called *flehmen*. He points his head up and curls back his upper lip. This blocks the male's *nostrils*, the openings to his nose. The flehmen behavior is important because ungulates, like all other mammals, have a passageway in the back of the throat that connects the nose and mouth. By closing his nostrils, the male traps the urine scent in this passageway so that it can be smelled. In some species, the male pushes the scent back toward the throat by pumping his tongue or moving his head back and forth.

If the scent is right, the male ungulate begins his courtship. The odor of the female's urine has given him the message that she is ready and willing to take him as a mate. If the scent is wrong, the male wanders off to find himself another female to sniff.

An African black rhinoceros pulls back its lips in a flehmen response after having smelled the urine of a female.

D. C. GORDON/
AMERICAN SOCIETY OF
MAMMOLOGISTS

a permanent connection

When a male deep-sea anglerfish finds a female, he gets really attached. In fact, the tiny male fish permanently fastens himself to his enormous female mate. This habit is particularly handy for anglers because they live over six thousand feet down, in the deep, dark depths of the ocean, where mates might be difficult to find.

A male deep-sea angler attaches himself soon after he leaves his egg. The two-inch male is thought to locate his two- to four-foot-long mate by scent. Once he finds her, the little angler uses sharp teeth to latch onto her body. Soon his mouth *fuses* to, or becomes part of, his mate's skin. He is now a parasite, completely dependent on the female. The little male is nourished by the female's blood and gets carried along wherever she swims. Because he no longer needs them, his eyes and digestive tract break down, or *degenerate*.

The combination of a tiny male and a huge female is unusual in the animal world. Often, as with geese, dogs, and house cats, both sexes are very similar in size. In species where there is a difference, like deer, peacocks, and gorillas, the male is almost always larger. Large, often colorful, males are partly the result of *sexual selection*. This means that females prefer them as mates. Large males may also have the job of protecting the female and young.

The male anglerfish doesn't need to look attractive to a female. He finds his mate and latches on. Then he has only one job: to produce sperm. The male remains small and parasitic throughout his life. The only parts that grow big are his reproductive organs. His lifetime work is simply to fertilize the female's eggs.

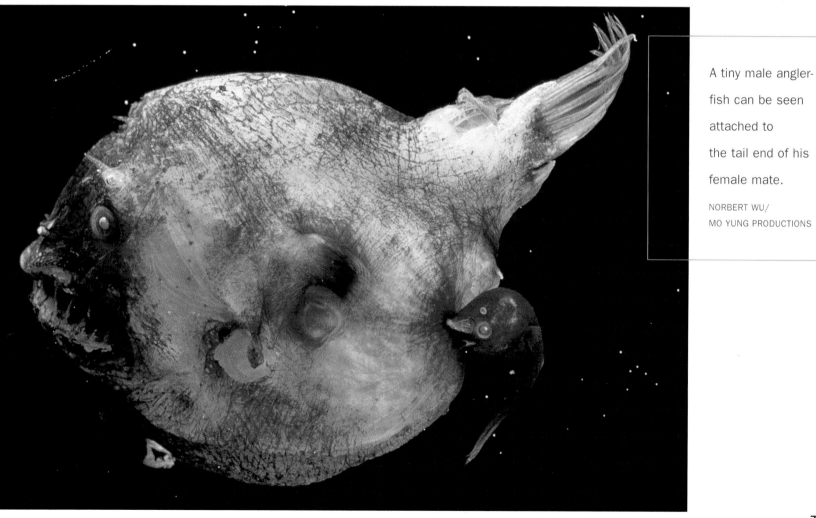

A tiny male angler-fish can be seen attached to the tail end of his female mate.

glossary

Brood parasite- An animal that lays its eggs in the nest of another animal, so that the other animal will raise its young.

Carnivore- An animal that eats meat.

Clotting- When blood cells clump together to form a plug. The plug is designed to stop up a cut or wound and keep it from bleeding.

Degenerate- When used to describe a part of the body such as the eye, it means that the body part breaks down and no longer works.

Excrete- To pass materials, such as wastes, out of the body.

Flehmen- A behavior in which a male animal curls back its lips and lifts its head in response to the scent of a female's urine. It is seen in animals with hooves, such as deer, horses, sheep, goats, and giraffes.

Fuse- When two things become permanently joined together.

Heat- A time when a female animal is ready and willing to mate with a male.

Herbivore- An animal that eats plants.

Hibernate- An animal withdraws from the outside world. This may occur when an animal is inside a cocoon maturing into its adult form. It may also occur when an animal enters a deep sleep during the winter or when conditions in the outside world are harsh.

Host- A living animal or plant that provides food for a parasitic animal or plant.

Incubate- To sit on eggs and warm them so that they will hatch.

Larva- A young, wingless insect or other immature invertebrate animal (an animal without a backbone).

Larvae- More than one larva.

Ligament- A tough band of tissue that holds bones together.

Mandibles- In insects, mandibles are the jaw or mouthparts.

Mandibular glands- Large sacs of chemicals found just below the mouth.

Metamorphosis- The changes that take place in an animal as it grows from an embryo to an adult. When insects go through metamorphosis they change from a larva to a pupa and from a pupa to a winged adult.

Mimic- An animal that copies the shape, colors, and behaviors of another animal. A mimic often uses its disguise to appear dangerous or inedible to predators.

Molt- When an animal molts, it sheds its skin or feathers and grows a new outer coat.

Nostrils- The holes that open into the nose.

Nymph- The young of certain insects, such as grasshoppers, which do not go through all the steps of metamorphosis. Nymphs often look like miniature adults.

Orbits- The cup-shaped parts of an animal's skull that hold its eyes.

Ovipositor- A pointed or needlelike structure found on the rear end of some female insects. It is used to deposit eggs.

Parasite- An animal that lives and feeds on or in another living organism and harms it in the process.

Parasitoid- A parasite that is only parasitic during its young or larval stage. Parasitoids destroy their hosts in the process of living off them.

Pheromone- A chemical produced by an animal that changes the behavior of other animals. Pheromones may be used to attract mates and warn other animals of danger.

Plankton- Very small animal-like and plantlike organisms that float in bodies of water. Many animals such as fish and insects feed on plankton.

Regurgitate- To throw up partly digested food.

Replete- A member of a honey ant colony that stuffs itself with food and stores the food in its own body. The replete's food is used by other colony members in times of need.

Roosting- When birds perch on a tree or a nest to rest or gather with other birds.

Sexual selection- Animals that are large, colorful, or in some way more attractive to members of the opposite sex get to mate more often. These animals thus have more offspring than others and pass on more of their traits to the next generation.

Symbiosis- When two different species of organisms live together. The relationship may be harmful to one of the organisms and beneficial to the other (parasitism), beneficial to just one organism and harmless to the other (commensalism), or beneficial to both organisms (mutualism).

Ungulate- A mammal with hooves. Ungulates include horses, cows, goats, sheep, and deer.

selected readings

Cheng, Thomas C., Ph.D. *The Biology of Animal Parasites.* Philadelphia and London: W.B. Saunders Company, 1964.

Conway, John R. "The Biology of Honey Ants." *The American Biology Teacher.* Vol. 48, no. 6 (September 1986).

Gertsch, Willis. *American Spiders.* New York: Van Nostrand Reinhold, 1979.

Grzimek, Bernard. *Grzimek's Animal Life Encyclopedia.* Vol. 1, 2, 5, and 9. New York: Van Nostrand Reinhold, 1972.

Holldobler, Bert, and E. O. Wilson. *Journey to the Ants.* Cambridge, Mass: The Belknap Press, Harvard University Press, 1994.

Lehane, M. J. *Biology of Blood-Sucking Insects.* London: HarperCollins Academic, 1991.

Lloyd, James. "Mimicry in the Sexual Signals of Fireflies." *Scientific American* 245, (1981): 138–145.

Schreiber, Ralph W., and Elizabeth Anne Schreiber. "Frigatebirds." In *Seabirds of Eastern North Pacific and Arctic Waters,*
    edited by Delphine Haley. Seattle, Washington: Pacific Search Press, 1984.

Street, Philip. *Animal Partners and Parasites.* New York: Taplinger Publishing, 1975.

Swan, Lester A., and Charles S. Papp. *The Common Insects of North America.* New York: Harper & Row, 1972.

Tanara, Milli. *The World of Amphibians and Reptiles.* New York: Abbeville Press, 1975.

Wallace, Robert A. *The Ecology and Evolution of Animal Behavior.* 2nd ed. Goodyear Publishing, 1979.

Wilkinson, Gerald. "Food Sharing in Vampire Bats." *Scientific American* 262 (1990): 76–79.

index